CELESTIAL DREAMS

5 ORIGINAL PIANO SOLOS BY NAOKO IKEDA

CONTENTS

ISBN 978-1-4234-3293-7

Visit Hal Leonard Online at
www.halleonard.com

Contact us:
Hal Leonard
7777 West Bluemound Road
Milwaukee, WI 53213
Email: info@halleonard.com

In Europe, contact:
Hal Leonard Europe Limited
42 Wigmore Street
Marylebone, London, W1U 2RN
Email: info@halleonardeurope.com

In Australia, contact:
Hal Leonard Australia Pty. Ltd.
4 Lentara Court
Cheltenham, Victoria, 3192 Australia
Email: info@halleonard.com.au

FOREWORD

SINCE ANCIENT TIMES, the stars in the night sky have been a symbol of hope to people everywhere, a sign that faraway dreams and secret ambitions are, perhaps, attainable. Time goes by, and the world around us keeps changing, but the stars above remain pure and mysterious. They remind us to savor each moment and to appreciate those closest to us. This collection of piano solos embraces that celestial philosophy and should be played with thoughts of the beautiful, hopeful stars that are steadfastly above us all.

With personal thanks to Teresa Ledford and Charmaine Siagian.

Naoko Ikeda

PERFORMANCE NOTES

The Sparkling Night Sky • *G Major* • *4/4* • *Andantino*

This piece was especially written for the many wonderful friends I've come to know around the world who have in some way exchanged kind thoughts, interesting ideas, and valuable friendships with me. The echoing phrases throughout the piece are intended to simulate these positive vibrations and unfold a very special universe of sound.

TIP: Make sure wrists and arms are relaxed, and play the slurs as elegantly as possible.

The Southern Cross • *C Major* • *6/8* • *Adagio*

The Southern Cross is a small but unique constellation, visible in the Southern Hemisphere, that points to the South Pole. Don't let the three staves of music confuse you. Imagine the top row as the Southern Cross, way up in the heavens. The next two rows represent the rhythmic and melodic essence of the piece. However, the coda (where you cross hands) is undeniably its heart and soul.

TIP: Top voicing is *essential* in the chord phrases. Try to ensure that each phrase is played differently.

The Shining North Star • *E-flat Major* • *3/4* • *Allegro brillante*

> Stormy, uncertain
> I look up, desperate for direction.
> *Shine like stars in a dark world...*
> I look forward, and slowly start walking.

The North Star is one of the brightest stars in the sky, and, similar to the Southern Cross pointing south, has been used for centuries as a guide towards north. *Shine like stars in a dark world…* is the motto for my alma mater here in Japan, written over 120 years ago by one of the American founders of the school. I have never forgotten these inspiring words.

In the introduction, imagine that you are one of the millions of stars shimmering above! Play the whole piece as expressively as you can, and incorporate your unique personality into your performance. Maintain control over the rhythm throughout, but especially at the end, which should be calm and tranquil.

TIP: Locate the climax of the piece—the Polestar!*

The B-flat octaves (located after the arpeggiated chords).

The Silver Boat • *A Minor* • *4/4* • *Andante con espressione*

There is a sad Japanese folk tale called *Taketori Monogatari* (The Tale of the Bamboo Cutter), which some believe is the oldest folk tale in history. One day, a childless bamboo cutter goes to work and stumbles upon a beautiful baby girl nestled in a golden bamboo stalk. Delighted, he rushes her home to his wife, and they name her Kaguya. They decide to raise and care for her as if she were their very own. Kaguya grows up to be a woman of exceptional beauty, and many seek her hand in marriage, including the emperor of Japan. She refuses them all without telling them why, but on clear moonlit nights she is especially sad, because she understands that she is a princess of the Moon, and it is her duty to return there one day. This piece is about the night she must return. A beautiful silver boat floats down silently from the moon and is waiting outside to carry Princess Kaguya home. Do you think she is desperate, calm, heartbroken, maybe a little frightened? Find the emotion in the music: express the strength of her spirit, the fate she cannot resist, and the sorrow of departure.

TIP: This is a sister piece to "Moon Flute," found in *Shoukei*, Book 1.

Shooting Stars in Summer • *A Major* • *4/4* • *Moderately slow, with wonder*

A night of shooting stars
Seen from different sides of distant shores
In time insight dawns:
No promises will be broken.

A night of shooting stars
Enveloping the colossal universe
And love sings blissful dreams
That it never wakes up from.

The style of this piece is a little more unusual than the other pieces in this collection. I chose the key of A Major because of its clear and open tone. Practice each phrase carefully and let the melody sing. The triplets symbolize the wonder of the shooting stars, and the next time you see one, make a special wish!

TIP: Work out the best fingering for the left hand before putting the piece together.

Translator: *Takako Teranishi*

The Sparkling Night Sky

for the Friends of Gillock Association of Japan

Naoko Ikeda

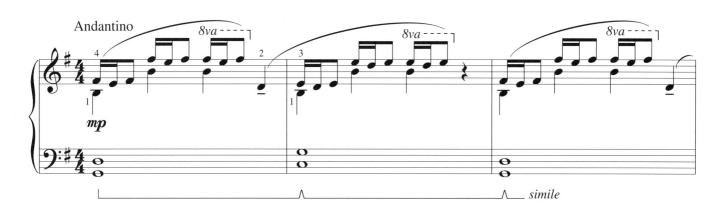

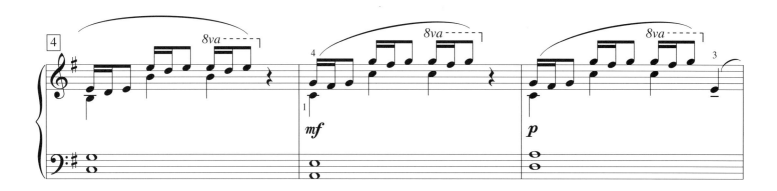

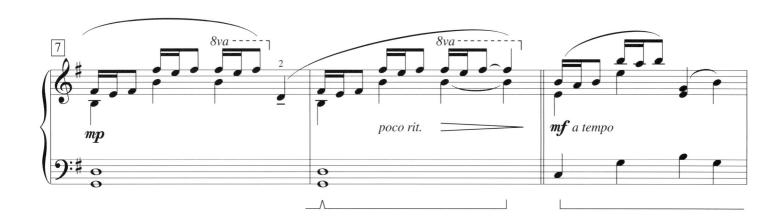

The Southern Cross

for Reika Yabuuchi

Naoko Ikeda

The Shining North Star

Written with fond memories of the Hokusei Gakuen Girls' High School Music Course

Naoko Ikeda

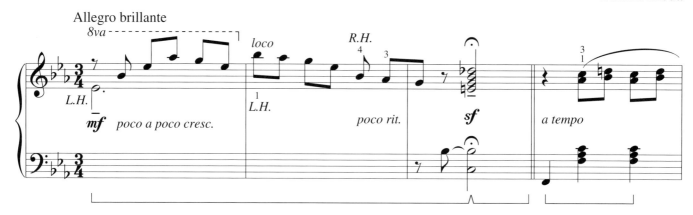

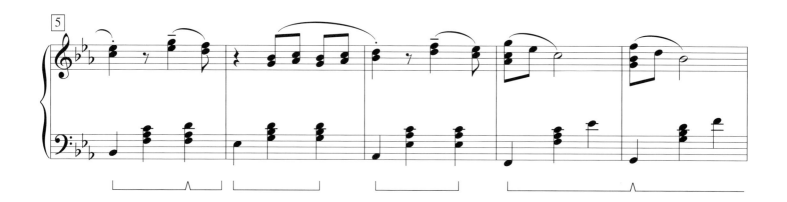

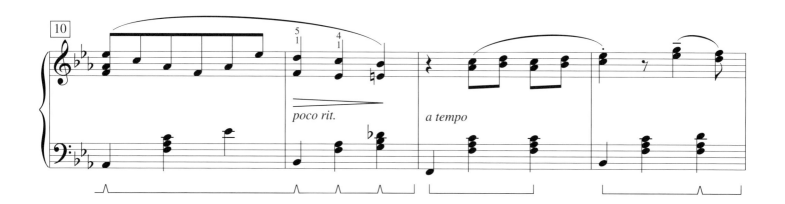

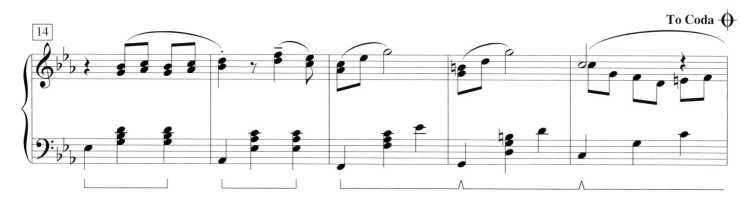

The Silver Boat

Naoko Ikeda

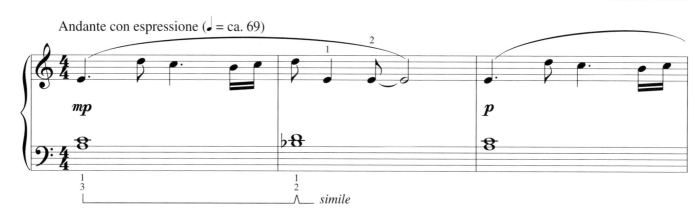

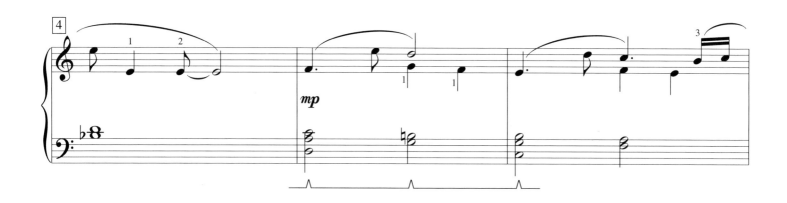

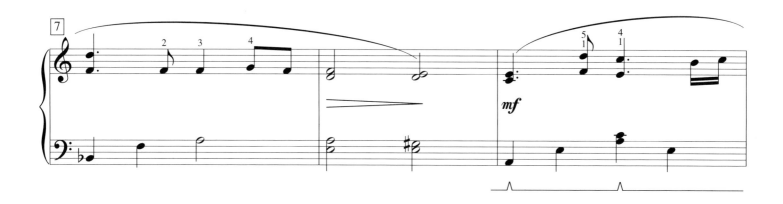

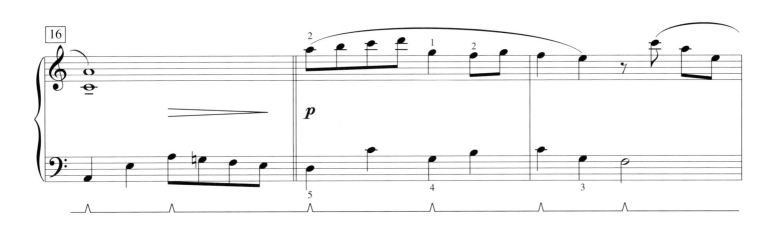

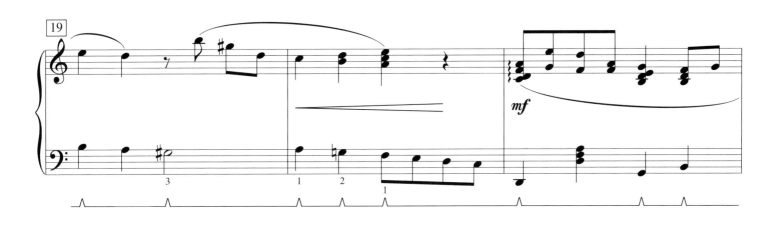

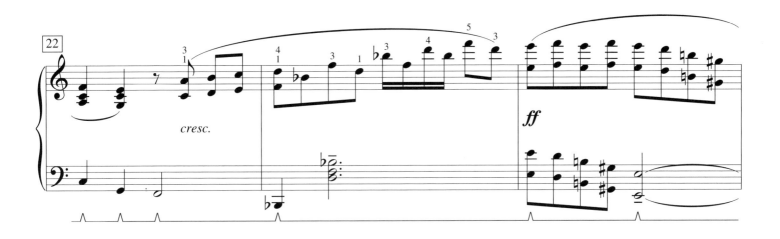

Shooting Stars in Summer

Naoko Ikeda

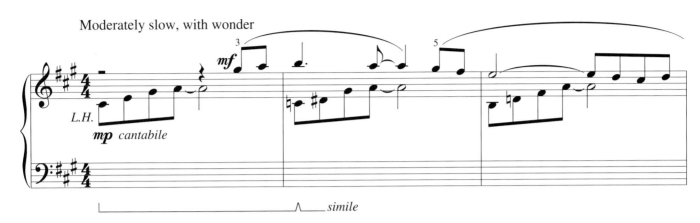

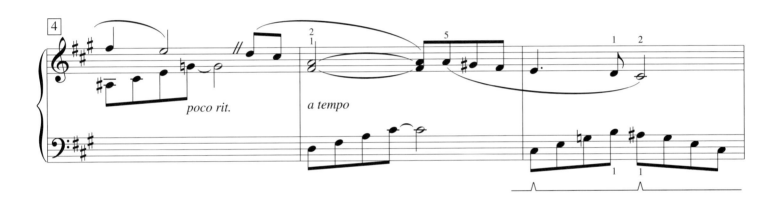

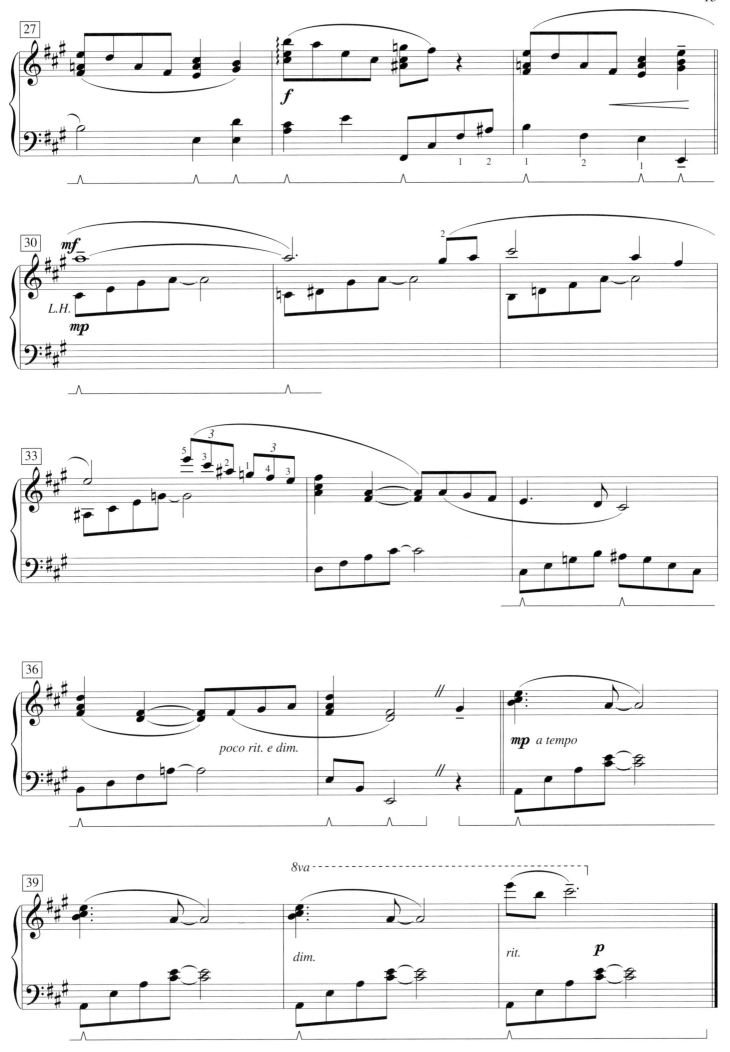

NAOKO IKEDA lives in Sapporo, Hokkaido in northern Japan, and is passionate about introducing the world to her country's essence through music. Influenced by classical music, jazz and pop, as well as the piano works of William Gillock, her own music reflects her diverse tastes with beauty, elegance, and humor. Ms. Ikeda is a proud graduate of the Hokusei Gakuen school system, and holds a piano performance degree from Yamaguchi College of Arts in Japan. She currently maintains an energetic schedule as both teacher and composer.